The Adventures of Charli

My Rescue Puppy

by Franca Caserta

Illustrations by Pat Achilles

Hope you enjoy my book and all my naughty Adventures. Always be kind to animals.

♡ Charli & Fran

For Carly Rose Whyte

"A dog has no use for fancy cars or big homes or designer clothes. Status symbol means nothing to him. A waterlogged stick will do just fine. A dog judges others not by their color or creed or class but by who they are inside. A dog doesn't care if you are rich or poor, educated or illiterate, clever or dull. Give him your heart and he will give you his. It was really quite simple, and yet we humans, so much wiser and more sophisticated, have always had trouble figuring out what really counts and what does not . . . I realized it was all right there in front of us, if only we opened our eyes. Sometimes it took a dog with bad breath, worse manners and pure intentions to help us see."

— John Grogan
Marley & Me

Special thank you to

Susan DeMilia of Circle Speech Services,
who gave me the idea to write a children's book
about my girl

My mom, who always inspires me every day
with her courage and strength

Pat Achilles, without whom I could not have done this.
You captured my girl beautifully in your illustrations.
I will never forget all that you did.

A portion of the proceeds from this book will benefit

Almost Home Dog Rescue

and

Ambrosia Foundation

I lost my girl Emma on April 26th, 2014. For 14 years, she'd wagged her tail every time I came home and I didn't think my heart would love another dog again. Then May 4th, 2014 came and I held Charli in my arms for the first time. I think she knew I would be a pushover when she looked into my eyes.

Charli was a rescue from South Carolina with Almost Home Dog Rescue and she made the trip all the way up to Pennsylvania to find me. To rescue a dog is to know pure joy and selflessness. If you've ever loved a dog, you know they give you their whole heart unconditionally. Rescues seem especially grateful for your love.

People don't tell you how hard it is to raise a puppy and I forgot all the mischief. Charli outdoes herself when it comes to mischief. These pages illustrate some of her naughty adventures.

A dog can be your hero when you need them, your eyes if you can't see, your companion when you are sad, your cuddle partner and your walking buddy. Dogs have many roles in people's lives and it is our job to love them.

I hope you enjoy the first year of my girl's naughty adventures and the love she has brought to my life.

My new rescue puppy.
I think she rescued me.

After knowing my girl for a day, meet Charli.
CC for short.

And why do I have to go in my crate when I can sit here...

One of life's simple moments
is watching your puppy
play in the snow
for the first time.

Pure joy and happiness.

My mom left me out two days
in a row by myself
and I didn't eat the house
or the cat

So I got a treat.

Happy St. Patrick's Day, everyone!
I got more Italian words today because
I dug a hole under the fence and got out.
She said her hair is going to look like mine soon—
and I don't mean brown like the mud yesterday.

Stay tuned for more Charli's Adventures
if my mom doesn't sell me on Ebay.

Happy Easter and Passover, everybody!
I found a snake outside today for my mom,
I don't think she liked it,
because she was screaming.
I asked to keep it and she said no,
then dressed me like this. ☺

I'm ... I ate my mom's paint samples
for her meeting tomorrow
so I'm in time out.
She said no TV for a week.

They were so colorful, I needed
to put them in my mouth.

I'm... well, let me think...
I was sleeping, yes I was sleeping on the pillow
yes, that blue pillow...
then it was like a noise,
then a big EXPLOSION
with all this white stuff
everywhere...

but I'm OK... see... 😊

I think I'm in trouble.
My mom yelled in Italian again.
I ate her pretty new flower.
I ripped the root right out and then ran in the house with the root. I don't know...
It was fun because she couldn't catch me.
She is putting me on the wall of shame,
She said...

isn't that like a trophy? :)

My mom's dryer broke, so she is hanging her clothes outside. It's like Disney World out here. I like getting real close to her so she thinks she can catch me but then I run.

She gave me another trophy — She said I'm the naughtiest dog ever.

I found this glove, well, I broke it off a stick
in my mom's garden.
The glove said "At Peace in My Garden."
I don't give her any more peace. ☺
I mean I did run back and forth with it,
while she was working, to show her...

that counts, right?

Um no, I'm not a hoarder.
Yes, these are my bones.
I hide them under the chair so
the cat doesn't eat them.
I do need all of them.
What if you forget to
feed me?
You did forget to feed me once,
and I could have eaten
my foot I was so hungry.

Can someone tell my mom to stop telling
my teacher all the naughty things I have done?
I understand a couple things but
to throw me under the bus just hurts.
I didn't mean to take the mozzarella cheese
from the counter and run outside with it.
but it was delicious.

... or peck the cat off the couch
while he is sleeping,
that guy is always sleeping.
I mean, go catch
a frisbee or something.
(·̫·)

My mom taught me a new command,
and that is "TRADE."
So when I take something like her shoe, doormat,
socks, butter, my Nonna's sandwich,
if I give it back I get a treat.
She said I am a Kleptomaniac.
She taught me the command,
not sure why she is so mad.
I am just smart, and I get
all the cookies I want now.

Everybody, this is Nikos, he's my best friend.
He's Greek and handsome.
We had a play date today.

We ran in the yard (I'm faster than him ☺)
and played fetch and tug-of-war.
I'm going swimming next week at his house.

It's cold out so I'm snuggling with my brother.
I like when he purrs...

If I promise not to dig any more holes
under your chair, so you don't fall in,
and I don't throw any more sand in your face,
can we stay?

Montauk, NY 2015
Stay tuned for more Charli Adventures...

Happy First Year to the Tsunami of my life.
Your happy little face makes things a little better every day.
You stole a piece of my heart
with my shoes,
remotes,
socks...

and I wouldn't have it any other way.

A Gallery of
Charli

These pictures of my girl are the original photos that inspired
my journey to this book.
The numbers on them correspond to the page illustrations.

10

11

12

13

14

15

28

29

30

31

32

33

34

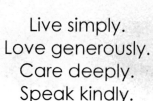

Live simply.
Love generously.
Care deeply.
Speak kindly.
Remember, if a dog was the teacher you would learn things like:
When loved ones come home, always run to greet them.
Allow the experience of fresh air and the wind in your face
to be pure Ecstasy.
Take naps.
Stretch before rising.
Run, romp, and play daily.
Thrive on attention and let people touch you.
Avoid biting when a simple growl will do.
On warm days, stop to lie on your back on the grass.
On hot days, drink lots of water and lie under a shady tree.
When you're happy, dance around and wag your entire body.
Delight in the simple joy of a long walk.
Be loyal.
Never pretend to be something you're not.
If what you want lies buried, dig until you find it.
When someone is having a bad day, be silent, sit close by,
and nuzzle them gently.
ENJOY EVERY MOMENT OF EVERY DAY!

— *Author unknown*

Made in the USA
San Bernardino, CA
24 March 2016